At School

Long Ago and Today

Lynnette R. Brent

Heinemann Library
Chicago, Illinois

© 2003 Heinemann Library
a division of Reed Elsevier Inc.
Chicago, Illinois

Customer Service 1-888-454-2279
Visit our website at
www.heinemannlibrary.com

Design by Herman Adler Design
Editorial Development by
Morrison BookWorks, LLC
Photo research by Carol Parden,
Image Resources
Printed and bound in the United States
of America, North Mankato, MN.

12 11 10
10 9 8 7 6 5 4 3 2

Library of Congress Cataloging-in-Publication Data
Brent, Lynnette R., 1965-
At school: long ago and today /
Lynnette R. Brent
    p. cm. -- (Times change)
Summary: An introduction to how education has changed in the past one hundred years, discussing how buildings and classrooms, books and lessons, recess and after school activities, and ways of getting to school are different.
Includes bibliographical references and index.
    ISBN 1-4034-4533-8 (lib. bdg.-hardcover) --
ISBN 978-1-4034-4539-1 (pbk)
1. Education, Elementary--United States--

122010
005992RP

History--Juvenile literature.
2. Schools--United States--History--Juvenile literature. [1. Education--History. 2. Schools--History.] I. Title. II. Series.
    LB1556.B74 2003
    372.973'09--dc21
                              2003011098

Acknowledgments
The author and publishers are grateful to the following for permission to reproduce copyright material: p. 5 William A. Bake/ Corbis; pp. 6, 28 H. Lebvre/ Retrofile.com; p. 7 Myrleen Ferguson/ PhotoEdit; pp. 8(t), 16(b), 24(b), 30(b-l) Bettmann/Corbis; pp. 8, 30(b-r) Laidlaw Education Services; p. 9 Steve Emery/Index Stock Imagery; pp. 10, 16(t) Corbis; p. 11 Richard Lord/The Image Works; p. 12 Library of Congress; p. 13 David R. Frazier/ Frazier Photolibrary; pp. 14, 20, 26 Brown Brothers; p. 15 Mug Shots/Corbis; p. 17 Tony Freeman/ PhotoEdit; 18(t) Museum of New Mexico; p. 19 O'Brien Productions/ Corbis; p. 21 Photodisc; pp. 22, 24(m) Culver Pictures; p. 23 Michael Newman/PhotoEdit; p. 25 Tom Carter/ PhotoEdit; p. 27 Will Hart/ PhotoEdit;
p. 29 Laura Dwight/Corbis

Cover photographs reproduced with permission of (t) Corbis, (b) Dan Tardiff/Corbis

Some words are shown in bold, **like this.**
You can find out what they mean by looking in the glossary.

Contents

Long Ago

Imagine that it is long ago. It is early in the morning and you are walking two miles to get to school. You will have to hurry. If you are late, you will have to stand outside until recess.

Is that the teacher ringing the bell? You had better run the rest of the way! School is about to begin.

This is what your school may have been like if you lived in the United States about 100 years ago. Let's see what school was like in the United States long ago.

This one-room schoolhouse was used long ago.

The School Year

Long ago, some schools were open for only four months out of the year. Other schools were open for six or eight months, and children attended when they could. Many children needed to work to help their families. Some children did chores on the farm, and some worked in factories in the city.

Children were often needed to help in the fields. They could not always go to school.

Times Change

What Changed in 1918?

By 1918, every state required that children had to attend school. It was the law.

Today, children do not work at home as much as they did in the past. Now, most schools last ten months, from early fall to late spring. Summer vacation lasts about two months. Some schools are held year-round, with short and long breaks throughout the year.

Today, children attend school even during the busy times on a farm.

Getting to School

Long ago, most students had to walk to get to school. Sometimes students had to walk an hour each way to school. Other students were lucky enough to have a horse. If they couldn't ride the horse, the horse could pull them to school in a wagon or sleigh.

Traveling to school on horseback was risky, but better than walking.

Times Change

What Changed in 1913?

In 1913, children began riding to school in school buses.

This school bus was used in 1913.

Today, some children still walk to school in their neighborhoods. Some ride their bicycles. Other children are driven to school in a car, van, or school bus. In cities, some students take a city bus or may even ride on a train.

The school bus is the safest and most popular way of getting to school.

School Buildings

One-room schoolhouses were common in the early 1900s.

Long ago, most schools were located in the country. These one-room schools served farm families who lived within four miles. Usually, there were fewer than 25 students in the whole school.

Times Change

What Changed in 1920?

As time passed, more and more people moved to cities for work. So, more and more schools were needed in cities.

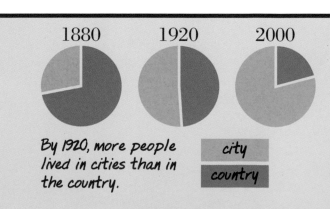

1880   1920   2000

By 1920, more people lived in cities than in the country.

city

country

Today, more schools are located in cities. Each school has many rooms and usually has more than 200 students. Sometimes, schools have more than 1,000 students. School buildings are larger to hold more children, more teachers, and other school workers.

Today, schools are larger and serve students from farther away.

The Students

Long ago, schools had one class for all students. Their ages ranged from six years to eighteen years old. All the students were taught together in the same room. Sometimes students who were four or five years old attended school with their older **siblings**. Often, the students would help each other learn their lessons.

Students of all ages were taught in one room.

Most students today are placed in classrooms based on their grade levels.

Today, most schools have students of one grade level in a classroom. For example, boys and girls who are six and seven years old are almost all in first grade. There are some schools today with multi-age classrooms. However, they don't have the wide range of ages that was common 100 years ago.

School Workers

Long ago, teachers spent ten hours a day at school. They often had to arrive early in the morning to build the fire that heated the schoolhouse. They were also responsible for keeping the schoolhouse clean. No one else worked in the school but the teacher.

This teacher is ringing his bell to let the students know school is ready to begin.

This librarian is helping students in the school library.

Today, teachers still work long hours, but there are many other school workers to help them. Principals make sure things run smoothly. Librarians help students find books to read and help with research projects. Custodians keep the school clean, and cafeteria workers serve breakfast and lunch to students.

The Classroom

Long ago, girls sat on one side of the room and boys sat on the other. They all sat on benches or at desks. Classrooms also had a teacher's desk, a blackboard, a flag, and maps.

The floors of the schools were made with wood, or sometimes even dirt! A **potbelly stove** or fireplace provided the heat. A water bucket was near the door with a **ladle** for drinking water.

A potbelly stove kept the students warm at school.

Times Change

What Changed in 1879?

Before Thomas Edison invented electricity in 1879, students were warmed by wood-burning stoves and studied with the light of gas lamps. By the early 1900s, most schools used electric heating systems and electric lights.

This is Thomas Edison in his lab.

Today, girls and boys sit next to each other in class. They might sit at desks or tables. Like classrooms long ago, many classrooms today also have a teacher's desk, blackboards, a flag, and maps.

Computer stations are often found in classrooms today. **Furnaces** provide warmth for students. Many schools also have air conditioning.

Compared to long ago, classrooms today are more comfortable.

Books and Materials

Long ago, students showed their work on small chalkboards like these.

Long ago, students used chalk and **slates** to do their work. Slates were small chalkboards students could use to practice spelling and math at their seats.

Books often had to be shared. Some teachers had books for students to read, but the classrooms were not full of bookshelves and materials.

Times Change

What Changed in 1880?

The type of pencil used today was invented in 1880. Before then, students wrote with chalk or pieces of lead.

Today, students have pencils, pens, and paper to do their work. They have many books to choose from. Many classrooms have large collections of books, and most schools today have a library. Students may also have textbooks for each school subject. In some schools, children can learn with computers.

Today, one of the ways children learn is by using the computer.

Lessons

Long ago, students learned their lessons through drills, reciting, and **memorizing.** During drills, teachers would ask each student questions, and students had to stand up to answer. Children memorized poems and had to recite them, or tell them by memory. In one-room schoolhouses, students would move on to a new reading book, not to a new class and grade.

Long ago, students studied reading, grammar, history, geography, science, and health. Students also learned "ciphering." That's what math was called!

Today, students study the same subjects as long ago, but they have more resources to help them learn their lessons.

Today, students have many resources to use that help them learn their lessons. Students can use textbooks, library books, and science **equipment.** Teachers still have discussions with students about what they are studying. Students often get to work with each other on projects.

Students today also take tests to show what they have learned.

Music, Art, and Physical Education

Long ago, art and music were mostly considered unnecessary. Students went to school to learn to read, write, and do math. During physical education, students might do exercises outside or stretch inside. The teacher led the exercises. Students did not exercise every day.

Students long ago did stretching activities for their physical education class.

Today, many schools have regular music and art classes. Music and art teachers may teach in the school's music room or art studio, or, instead, teach students in the regular classroom. Most schools also have physical education classes every day. These classes are located in a gym or outside on the playground.

Today, students learn games such as volleyball during their physical education class.

Lunchtime

Long ago, students had an hour for lunch. Some went home for lunch. Those who stayed at school would eat either outside or in the classroom. The students would bring their lunch with them in buckets or cloth napkins. They often brought leftovers from last night's dinner, or bread smeared with lard. Lucky students had a piece of chocolate cake or a piece of homemade pie.

Students brought their lunches from home.

Times Change

What Changed in 1946?

The National School Lunch Act began in 1946. Before then, few schools offered lunch at school. In 1946, schools were required to offer lunch to students.

Many children ate hot lunches at school.

Today, most students eat lunch in the cafeteria.

Today, most students have about 30 minutes for lunch. Many students still bring their lunch from home in paper bags or lunch boxes. Lunch may also be food that is packaged rather than homemade. Some students eat food provided by the school cafeteria.

Recess

Long ago, children had a short recess in the morning and a longer recess after lunch. There were no slides or other playground **equipment,** just open fields around the school building. Children played ball games, tag, or other games such as "Duck, Duck, Goose."

Children often played leap frog at recess.

Today, recess is still a time to have fun during the school day.

Today, children may have recess after lunch or at another time during the day. They play on playground equipment or baseball diamonds. They also play games such as tag and hopscotch.

After School

After school, children had chores to do at home.

Long ago, students may have had a long walk home. Once they arrived at home, they had to do chores, work on the farm, or work in factories. There was very little time for studying and doing homework.

Many families long ago had to pay for their children to attend school. Some children had to work in exchange for their schooling.

Times Change

What Changed in 1850?

By 1850, public schools were free to attend. Before then, students had to either pay to attend school or work in exchange for their schooling.

Today, children do many different things after school. Some children are involved in after-school sports or clubs. Some sports and clubs meet at school. Students might go to a park district or other program with other children. Some children visit with friends or play after school.

Most children have homework to do to help them prepare for the next day of school.

You have seen how schools have changed over time. Schools have become larger, the school year is longer, and teachers have different jobs. Students write with different tools and learn in classrooms that look different.

But schools are the same in some ways, too. Students still attend school to learn new things. Teachers still work to help students learn new subjects. And many children still walk to school each day.

Times Change

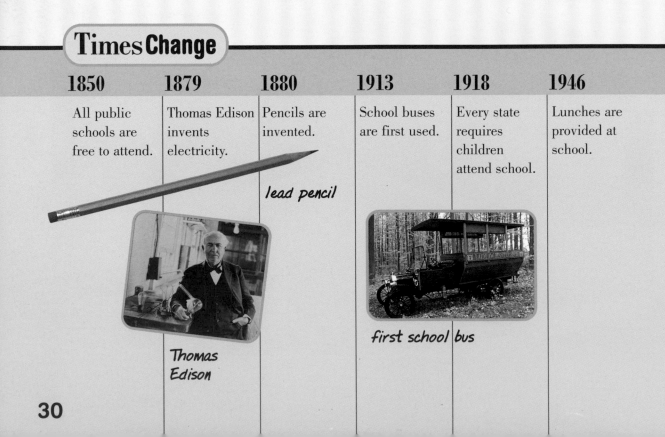

1850	1879	1880	1913	1918	1946
All public schools are free to attend.	Thomas Edison invents electricity.	Pencils are invented.	School buses are first used.	Every state requires children attend school.	Lunches are provided at school.

lead pencil

Thomas Edison

first school bus

Glossary

equipment objects and materials used to help with learning

furnace machine used to heat buildings

ladle deep-bowled, long-handled spoon

memorizing remembering

potbelly stove stove with a rounded or bulging body

siblings people who have the same parents

slate tablet used for writing on

More Books to Read

Carney, Rita Reber. *Me & My One-Room Schoolhouse.* Rita T. Carney. 2000.

Pringle, Laurence. *One Room School.* Boyds Mills Press. Honesdale, Pennsylvania, 1998.

Ask an older reader to help you read these books:

Bial, Raymond. *One-Room School.* Houghton Mifflin. Boston, 1999.

Kalman, Bobbie. *A One-Room School.* Crabtree Publishing. New York, 1994.

Index